INTRODUCING DINOSAURS

TRICERATOPS

BY SUSAN H. GRAY · ILLUSTRATED BY ROBERT SQUIER

The Child's World

Published in the United States of America by The Child's World®
1980 Lookout Drive • Mankato, MN 56003-1705
800-599-READ • www.childsworld.com

ACKNOWLEDGMENTS
The Child's World®: Mary Berendes, Publishing Director
The Design Lab: Kathleen Petelinsek, Art Direction and Design;
Victoria Stanley and Anna Petelinsek, Page Production
Editorial Directions: E. Russell Primm, Editor; Lucia Raatma, Copy Editor;
Dina Rubin, Proofreader; Tim Griffin, Indexer

PHOTO CREDITS
©Alphtran/Dreamstime.com: cover, 2–3; ©A.J. Copley/Visuals Unlimited,
Inc.: 4; ©Kevin Schafer/Corbis: 8–9; ©Francois Gohier/Photo Researchers,
Inc.: 14; ©David Muench/Corbis: 16–17; ©Annie Griffiths Belt/Corbis:
17 (top); ©Richard T. Nowitz/Photo Researchers, Inc.: 18–19; ©Reuters
NewMedia, Inc./Corbis: 19 (right)

LIBRARY OF CONGRESS CATALOGING-IN-PUBLICATION DATA
Gray, Susan Heinrichs.
   Triceratops / by Susan H. Gray; illustrated by Robert Squier.
      p. cm.—(Introducing dinosaurs)
   Includes bibliographical references and index.
   ISBN 978-1-60253-243-4 (lib. bound: alk. paper)
   1. Triceratops—Juvenile literature. I. Squier, Robert, ill. II. Title. III. Series.
   QE862.O65G74622 2009
   567.915'8—dc22   2009001632

TABLE OF CONTENTS

What was *Triceratops*? 4

What did *Triceratops* look like? 7

How did *Triceratops* spend its time? 11

What if another dinosaur attacked? 12

How do we know about *Triceratops*? 16

Where have *Triceratops* bones been found? 20

Who finds the bones? 21

Glossary 22

Books and Web Sites 23

About the Author and Illustrator 24

Index 24

WHAT WAS TRICERATOPS?

Triceratops (try-SAYR-ah-tops) was a dinosaur that lived long ago. Its name means "three-horned face." Just look at that face! *Triceratops* has the perfect name!

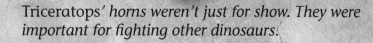

Triceratops' horns weren't just for show. They were important for fighting other dinosaurs.

5

WHAT DID *TRICERATOPS* LOOK LIKE?

Triceratops was a big, chunky dinosaur. It weighed more than 250 first-grade children! It had tough skin. It stood on four sturdy legs. It had a thick, heavy tail.

Triceratops *was gigantic! Many other dinosaurs were also very large.*

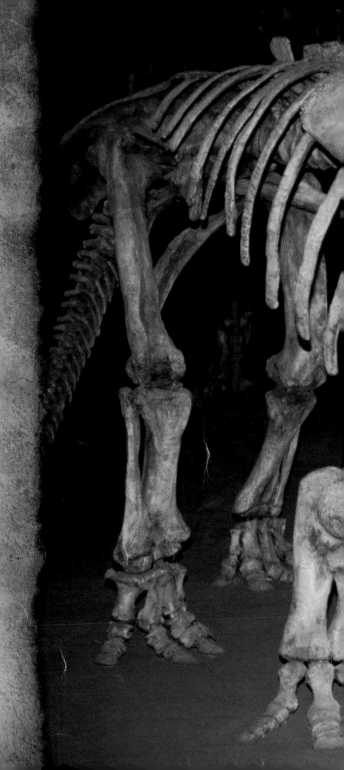

Triceratops had a gigantic head. It had a hard beak instead of lips. It had only one horn on its snout. It had two bigger horns above its eyes. The back of the head spread out like a **shield**. That shield is called a **frill**.

Triceratops had no teeth in the front of its mouth. It had many teeth farther back. *Triceratops* ate tough plants. It clipped off branches with its beak. Its teeth shredded everything.

Triceratops' head was good for two things. Its shape was perfect for eating plants and defending against attackers.

HOW DID *TRICERATOPS* SPEND ITS TIME?

Triceratops did not spend much time alone. Instead, it stayed with its **herd**. Together, the dinosaurs looked for food and water. They stopped to eat and to sleep.

They also stopped to lay eggs. Babies hatched and grew up in the herd. They felt safe with all the bigger *Triceratops* around.

Living in a herd helped Triceratops *to avoid attacks from other dinosaurs.*

WHAT IF ANOTHER DINOSAUR ATTACKED?

Triceratops was not a fierce **predator**.

It did not look for fights. But if another

dinosaur attacked, it was ready.

Triceratops *was not an easy target. Its horns and frill provided great protection.*

13

14

Triceratops would turn and face its **enemy**. The frill made *Triceratops* look huge and scary. Then *Triceratops* might have stomped its feet and snorted. Others in the herd might have joined in. That should have frightened any predator away! If not, *Triceratops* had one last trick. It could ram an attacker with its horns!

If Triceratops' massive size didn't frighten off a predator, a painful poke from its horns certainly did.

HOW DO WE KNOW ABOUT *TRICERATOPS*?

Triceratops lived millions of years ago. Some of its **fossils** are still around. **Scientists** have found its bones and teeth. They have even found its bone beds. These are places with many *Triceratops* **skeletons** together.

This bone bed (right) at Dinosaur National Monument in Colorado is one of the best in the world. Scientists carefully clean bones found near Orchard, Nebraska (far right).

The bone beds help scientists learn more about what *Triceratops'* life was like. Because of the fossils found there, we know how Triceratops lived and what it ate.

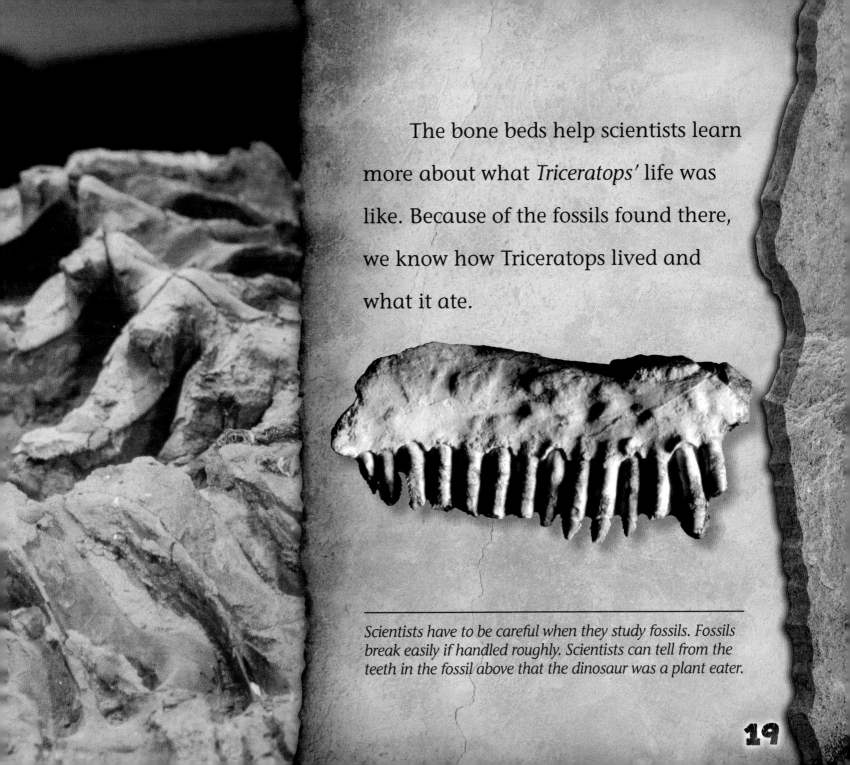

Scientists have to be careful when they study fossils. Fossils break easily if handled roughly. Scientists can tell from the teeth in the fossil above that the dinosaur was a plant eater.

WHERE HAVE TRICERATOPS BONES BEEN FOUND?

Alberta, Canada

Montana

Saskatchewan, Canada

North Dakota

Wyoming

NORTH AMERICA

South Dakota

Colorado

EUROPE

ASIA

Atlantic Ocean

Pacific Ocean

AFRICA

SOUTH AMERICA

Indian Ocean

AUSTRALIA

Map Key

Where *Triceratops* bones have been found

Southern Ocean

WHO FINDS THE BONES?

Fossil hunters find dinosaur bones. Some fossil hunters are scientists. Others are people who hunt fossils for fun. They go to areas where dinosaurs once lived. They find bones in rocky places, in mountainsides, and in deserts.

When fossil hunters discover dinosaur bones, they get busy. They use picks to chip rocks away from the fossils. They use small brushes to sweep off any dirt. They take pictures of the fossils. They also write notes about where the bones were found. They want to remember everything!

Fossil hunters use many tools to dig up fossils. It is very important to use the right tools so the fossils do not get damaged.

GLOSSARY

enemy (*EN-ah-mee*) An animal's enemy is someone or something that wants to attack it.

fossils (*FOSS-ullz*) Fossils are preserved parts of plants and animals that died long ago.

frill (*FRIL*) A frill on a dinosaur was a part of the head or neck that spread out very wide.

herd (*HURD*) A herd is a group of animals that travels together.

predator (*PRED-ah-tur*) A predator is an animal that hunts and eats other animals.

scientists (*SY-un-tists*) Scientists are people who study how things work through observations and experiments.

shield (*SHEELD*) A shield is a piece of armor used for protection.

skeletons (SKEL-uh-tunz) Skeletons are the sets of bones in peoples' or animals' bodies.

Triceratops (*try-SAYR-ah-tops*) *Triceratops* was a dinosaur with three horns on its head.

BOOKS

Bentley, Dawn. *Watch Out, Triceratops!*
Norwalk, CT: Little Soundprints, 2004.

Lorbiecki, Marybeth. *Triceratops*.
Vero Beach, FL: Rourke Publishing, 2007.

My Terrific Dinosaur Book.
New York: DK Publishing, 2008.

Parker, Steve. *Dinosaurus: The Complete Guide to Dinosaurs*.
New York: Firefly Books, 2003.

WEB SITES

Visit our Web site for lots of links about *Triceratops*:

CHILDSWORLD.COM/LINKS

Note to Parents, Teachers, and Librarians: We routinely verify our Web links to make sure they are safe, active sites—so encourage your readers to check them out!

INDEX

babies, 11
beak, 8
bone beds, 16, 19
bones, 16, 19, 20, 21

eggs, 11
eyes, 8

feet, 15
fighting, 12, 15
food, 8, 11
fossils, 16, 19, 21
frill, 8, 15

head, 8
herds, 11, 15, 19
horns, 4, 8, 15

legs, 7

map, 20

name, 4

plants, 8
predators, 15

size, 7, 15
skin, 7
sleeping, 11
snorting, 15

tail, 7
teeth, 8, 16
tools, 21

water, 11
weight, 7

ABOUT THE AUTHOR

Susan Gray has written more than ninety books for children. She especially likes to write about animals. Susan lives in Cabot, Arkansas, with her husband, Michael, and many pets.

ABOUT THE ILLUSTRATOR

Robert Squier has been drawing dinosaurs ever since he could hold a crayon. Today, instead of using crayons, he uses pencils, paint, and the computer. Robert lives in New Hampshire with his wife, Jessica, and a house full of dinosaur toys. *Stegosaurus* is his favorite dinosaur.